Egyptian cults and sanctuaries on Delos

Hélène BRUN-KYRIAKIDIS

ÉCOLE FRANÇAISE D'ATHÈNES
ΓΑΛΛΙΚΗ ΣΧΟΛΗ ΑΘΗΝΩΝ

Preliminary note

The initials *IG* and *ID* used in the sources cited at the end of the book refer to the corpus of the *Inscriptiones Graecae* and the *Inscriptions de Délos*. The numbers preceded by the letter A identify the statues and reliefs held at the Archaeological Museum of Delos.

The ★ symbol indicates a monument located on the maps of the inside covers.

The letters identifying the monuments of Sarapieia A and C on plans 12, 24 and 26 correspond to those used in Ph. Bruneau, J. Ducat, *Guide de Délos* (2005).

Chronology

All dates are BC unless otherwise specified.

317–167: Period of Independence in Delos, following the first Athenian domination.

early 4th century: appearance of the deity Sarapis in Alexandria (Egypt) and Hellenisation of the goddess Isis.

late 4th century: beginning of the spread of Isiac cults beyond Egypt.

167: beginning of the second Athenian domination. The Roman Senate declares the port of Delos tax-free in favour of Athens and the Delians are driven from the island.

88: first Delian 'catastrophe'. Supported by a number of Greek cities hostile to Roman taxation, King Mithridates Eupator wins a series of battles against Rome; his troops seize Delos and the island is ransacked.

69: second Delian 'catastrophe'. Under Athenodorus' command, Mithridates' allied pirates once again sack the city. Delian trading enters a sharp decline and never recovers.

Introduction

Renowned to this day for its Sanctuary of Apollo, the island of Delos was a flourishing trading port in antiquity that drew both Greeks and foreigners to its shores for commercial purposes. Many exotic deities – some hailing from the east and others, introduced by the Italian community, from the west – were worshipped on the island. Among these foreign divinities, the Egyptian gods figured prominently, and their first appearance can be dated from the 3rd century, before the population explosion linked to the Roman Senate's decision to make the island a free port in 167.

The spread of Egyptian-Greek cults beyond the Nile Valley favoured the worship of the goddess Isis, hence the use of the term 'Isiac cults' when referring to them. While the goddess was the object of great devotion on Delos as elsewhere, it was actually the god Sarapis who was at the centre of a pantheon forming a triad with Isis and Anubis, joined by Harpocrates, Ammon and Osiris. The Delians dedicated three sanctuaries to Sarapis. Their unique layouts and the inscriptions and furniture they contained provide valuable information on the island's cultic practices. Elsewhere, signs of private devotion have also been uncovered. Excavations in the houses and the necropolis of Rheneia have yielded elements of adornments, statuettes and scarabs. This series of *isiaca* or *aegyptiaca*, as they are sometimes called, make Delos one of the richest Greek sites in terms of information on Isiac cults in the Hellenistic period.

Gods from Egypt

Particularly venerated on Delos, the god Sarapis is a composite deity consisting of certain Osirian traits mixed with features borrowed from Zeus and Hades. In Egypt his cult was developed by the first Ptolemies, the Greek rulers who took control of the country after its conquest by Alexander, and who founded a very active Sarapieion in Alexandria. The name 'Sarapis' appears to have come from the Egyptian *Osor-Api*, 'the Osiris Apis', signifying the god Apis after his death when he was worshipped in the form of a bull in his Memphis sanctuary. Towards the end of the 4th century, the cults of Sarapis and Isis began to spread beyond the Nile Valley, and Sarapieia and Iseia were founded in a number of Greek cities, including Athens, Eretria, Rhodes and Delos.

THE ARRIVAL OF SARAPIS

A well-known text referred to as the 'Chronicle of the Sarapieion' explains the circumstances connected to the appearance of the cult of Sarapis on Delos. Engraved on a votive column found in Sarapieion A (1) and reading like an apologia, this long inscription tells a story that must be regarded with some suspicion. The first section, written in prose by the priest Apollonius, is a succinct account of how his grandfather Apollonius brought a statue of Sarapis to Delos to celebrate the cult in his own home (box 1). He goes on to stipulate that, having become a priest like his father before him, he built a sanctuary for his god. This shrine became the subject of a trial, which he explains he won with the help of the deity who silenced his accusers. The second part of the inscription tells a fuller, versified version of the same story.

The realistic details concerning the purchase of the land and the construction of the sanctuary make this account of the god's installation in his Delian establishment particularly vivid. It describes how the priest Apollonius consulted the property advertisements displayed, as has been established, in the main entrance of the Agora of the Delians (★), and how he purchased land indicated by the god, of rather relative quality as it happens, as it is described as a plot 'full of dirt'. Such a detail emphasises, by contrast, the grandeur of the god and the infamy of his enemies. Apollonius is careful not to reveal the reason for the accusation against him, he only recounts that Sarapis helped him win the trial.

The Chronicle of the Sarapieion relates, in prose and then in verse, the arrival of the god Sarapis on Delos and the miracle he accomplished to save his priest Apollonius, who became the subject of a trial after the construction of the sanctuary.

Apollonius the priest had (this text) inscribed in accordance with an injunction from the god. For Apollonius, my grandfather, who was an Egyptian from the priestly class came from Egypt with his god, and continued to celebrate the cult in accordance with ancestral tradition; he lived, it is thought, to the age of 97. My father Demetrius, succeeded him and worshipped the gods in the same way; because of his piety, he was honoured by the god with a bronze statue which is dedicated in the temple of the god. He lived 61 years. When I inherited the sacred objects and devoted myself carefully to his cult, the god told me in my sleep that a Sarapeum of his own must be dedicated to him and that he must not be as before in a rented building; he said he would find a spot himself where he should be set and that he would point it out. And this is what happened. Now this spot was full of dirt, and was advertised for sale on a little notice (displayed) in the passage to the agora. As the god wanted this the purchase was completed and the sanctuary was rapidly built in six months. And when some men joined against us and the god, and introduced a public suit against the sanctuary and me, involving a penalty or a fine, the god promised to me in my sleep that we would be victorious. Now that the trial is completed and we have won a victory worthy of the god, we praise the gods and repay them adequate thanks.

IG XI, 1299, l. 1-28

Translation: M. M. Austin, *The Hellenistic World From Alexander to the Roman Conquest* (1981).

(1) *The Chronicle of the Sarapieion*

This aretalogy* of Sarapis dates back to the end of the 3rd or the beginning of the 2nd century and is thought to coincide with the foundation of Sarapieion A. The god's arrival on the island is situated during the lifetime of the author of the Chronicle's grandfather, i.e., around the first half of the 3rd century. The text specifies that at the age of 97 Apollonius the Egyptian passed on the priesthood to his son Demetrius, who, dying at 61, left his appointment to his son Apollonius, our sanctuary builder.

According to the Chronicle, Apollonius the Elder, who introduced the cult of Sarapis into Delos, was an Egyptian priest from Memphis. Was he a member of the famed Sarapeum of Memphis' sacerdotal class before settling in Delos? Why did he leave Memphis? Is his name the translation of an Egyptian anthroponym formed from Horus, who the Greeks equated with Apollo? Rather than a native Egyptian, he is sometimes regarded as an Egyptian Greek, or perhaps even a Hellenomemphite, the descendants of Greek mercenaries who entered the service of the pharaoh Psamtik before settling in Memphis, as reported by Herodotus (*The Histories*, II, 154). All in all, Apollonius' personality, history and motivations remain enigmatic. The arrival, however, of the Isiac gods on Delos is early in comparison to other foreign cults that didn't reach the island until after 167, when commerce developed under the rule of Athens.

THE CULT OFFICIALISED

The inscriptions have revealed that the god Sarapis was officially adopted by the city-state of Delos around 190–180. It can therefore be surmised that the devotion the deity aroused had become fairly popular by that time. The seat of this public cult, which prospered throughout the 2nd century, was Sarapieion C, while Sarapieion A remained a private sanctuary, administered by the descendants of Apollonius the Egyptian.

Once the god was accepted into the civic pantheon, the Sarapis priests who officiated in Sarapieion C were chosen from among Delian citizens and from 167, among Athenians. The sanctuary was placed under the supervision of the official administrators of public cults: hieropes throughout the Independent period and magistrates 'in charge of sacred affairs' during the second Athenian domination. They established the periodic list of divine possessions, in the form of inventories (some of which have survived today), kept the accounts, and financed a number of constructions and restorations. From this point on, the income generated by Sarapis supplemented that of Delos' 'sacred fund', *i.e.*, the Apollo fund. This formalisation of the cult of Sarapis proves that it was neither a 'sect' nor a minority or exotic religion. For the inhabitants of 2nd century Delos, Sarapis and his circle formed an integral part of the religious landscape, and although today we may call them foreigners or Orientals, they were almost certainly not perceived as such by their followers.

A COMPLEX PANTHEON

Although Sarapis was not the only god from the Egyptian pantheon to be celebrated on Delos, he was certainly the central figure. In the inscriptions, each of the three Delian sanctuaries is designated as 'Sarapieion' and the priests who officiated at the public sanctuary bear the title of 'priest of Sarapis'. Sarapis, however, formed a triad with Isis and Anubis and was usually invoked concomitantly. This triad is named in most of the dedications in all three sanctuaries from the cult's very beginnings. From the middle of the 2nd century, Harpocrates, the Hellenised version of the Egyptian god Horus, was regularly added to this trio. The list of the gods of the Sarapieia evolved as the faithful frequenting the shrines made personal devotions; and it is essentially through these individual dedications that their existence is known. Some were frequently invoked, while others more rarely; some are extremely well known, while others appear to be local deities; some are Egyptian, while others bear Greek names, possibly translated from Egyptian. All were '*synnaoi*' (who share the same temple) or '*symbomoi*' (who share the same altar) gods. The richest pantheon is found in Sarapieion C, the largest of the sanctuaries.

Delos' Egyptian gods also vary in character and scope of action. Sarapis and Isis were both 'saviour gods' who intervened in the destinies of humans. The images of ears occasionally dedicated to them testifies to their ability to listen and answer prayers (2). Sarapis also appeared to his followers in dreams to convey his wishes.

(2)

Egyptian cults and sanctuaries on Delos

He ordered the priest Apollonius to purchase the land for the future Sarapieion A (box 1) in a dream, and other dedications also bear witness to his directives: the offerings they commemorate were made 'in compliance with an order' (box 3, p. 38) or sometimes 'in compliance with a dream'.

Healing gods also had an important place in the Sarapieia, including Asclepius and Hygieia, Heracles Apallaxikakos ('who drives away illness'), and the Sarapis of Canopus, a town in the Nile Delta and home to a sanctuary renowned for its cures. The Isiac gods protected sailors and safeguarded their followers from the perils of the sea. In Delos, Isis was sometimes invoked as Isis Euploia ('who protects navigation') and a relief exists representing the goddess inventing the sail (Isis Pelagia: 3). Other gods who protected seafarers, such as the Dioscuri (Castor and Pollux), were also associated with these Egyptian cults. Generally speaking, the Isiac gods were givers of good fortune and Isis is often depicted holding a cornucopia (4), a symbol which also appears on seal imprints discovered in

(3)

(4)

(5)

Sarapieion C (5). There were therefore many reasons to visit Sarapis, Isis or the gods of their circle, and the diversity of their powers also explains the success they enjoyed on the island.

On Delos, these deities' representations were clearly Hellenised. Nothing in the appearance of the statuette of an enthroned god found in Sarapieion B (6), for example, evokes exoticism. Although the head and arms are missing, the position

(6)

Egyptian cults and sanctuaries on Delos

of the shoulder suggests that the raised right hand held a sceptre. Another statuette (A 1990 + A 2003) discovered in the same sanctuary presents a bearded god, seated and draped in a cloak revealing part of his torso and his right shoulder. His feet rest on a stool bearing the name of a priest, but the actual dedication is lost. As the god is portrayed with none of his usual attributes, only the context in which these two objects were discovered suggests they are images of Sarapis.

(7)

Isis was also represented as a Greek deity. In Sarapieion C, a statue of the goddess still standing in her temple, though missing her head and arms (7), clearly presents her *à la Grecque*, draped in a tunic (*chiton*) and wrapped in a cloak (*himation*). More exotic images of the Egyptian gods of Delos however have also survived. Dorsal pillar figurines represent Isis in keeping with Egyptian aesthetic canons (8) and reliefs and seal imprints depicting the Hathoric crown* plainly evoke her origins (9). A statuette of Anubis portrayed with the head of a jackal, discovered in Sarapieion A, also testifies to eastern influence (10). Although the god's body is swathed in a Greek form of drapery, his canine head clearly assimilates the statuette to the Nile Valley's theriomorphic* representations. Other similar images are known only from the inscriptions: an inventory dating from 145–144 mentions a statue of a falcon, which may possibly have been an image of Horus. Such examples, however, are few, and, like the Greek deities, the gods of the Sarapieia were generally anthropomorphic.

(8)

(9)

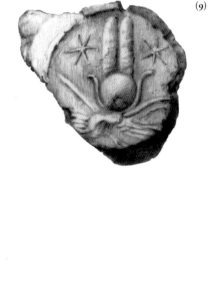

Egyptian cults and sanctuaries on Delos

Three sanctuaries to visit

The island of Delos has retained significant material evidence of the Egyptian cults. The archaeological exploration of the island at the end of the 19th and early 20th centuries brought to light no less than three sanctuaries devoted to Sarapis. They are all located in the same district, the 'Inopos' Quarter, named after the island's main water course which flowed through this area. In antiquity, the Inopos was seen as a resurgence of the Nile, which may explain the Egyptian gods' presence in this part of the town. It may also be supposed that as this district was not as heavily urbanised as the Theatre Quarter or the immediate surroundings of the Sanctuary of Apollo, it was easier for new gods to find their place. The first excavations took place in Sarapieion C. Its location was known from the beginning of the 19th century, when on a visit to Delos in 1810, Charles Robert Cockerell copied inscriptions mentioning the Egyptian gods. During the first campaign in 1880, archaeologists excavated only a limited portion of the monuments and mistook three distinct sanctuaries for one which they called 'the sanctuary of the foreign gods'. The Heraion (★) was taken for the temple of Sarapis and the boundary between the Syrian (★) and Egyptian (★) sanctuaries was not ascertained.

Excavations resumed in Sarapieion C in 1909 and 1910, and a year later (11) the sanctuary was identified and its boundaries with the Heraion and the Sanctuary of Atargatis, the Syrian goddess, were established. Also in 1910, Pierre Roussel, who had directed the excavations on the 'Terrace of the Foreign Deities', discovered

Sarapieion B, located below the Syrian sanctuary. In 1911, Johannès Pâris, who was excavating in the Inopos valley, discovered Sarapieion A and the column bearing the Chronicle inscription. In 1916 Pierre Roussel published a history of Egyptian cults on Delos, together with all the related inscriptions. He was also responsible for designating the three Sarapieia by the letters A, B and C, which he believed corresponded to their chronology. The dates of their construction, however, remain hypothetical, as does the order in which they were built.

SARAPIEION A

Sarapieion A (★) is therefore considered to be the oldest of the three sanctuaries (12 and 13). Its simple architecture consists of walls built using local materials which were originally rendered to conceal the masonry's irregular appearance. A rough staircase opened in the north wall provided access to the sanctuary, located below the street that leads to the Inopos reservoir (★).

The sanctuary's buildings, erected around a small courtyard paved with large slabs of gneiss (12, **B**), are clearly visible from both the northern door and the south bank of the Inopos (14). On the east side, a temple – a simple *cella** (**A**) – is preceded by a staircase. In its basement, a semi-underground room (a crypt), whose door is situated on the south side of the temple, provides access to water from a large reservoir supplied by the groundwater (15). Today this reservoir runs from west to east for about 4.5 metres, but as its eastern wall has collapsed, its

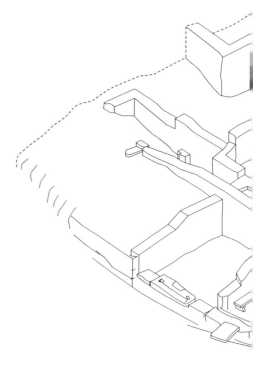

exact dimensions and capacity remain unknown. Its water could be drawn no doubt not only from the crypt, but also from another smaller, square-shaped well cut into the temple's eastern wall.

Opening on to the courtyard at the northern end are two rooms situated on either side of the main staircase. The first of these, to the northeast, occupies a raised terrace and two of its walls feature niches built of masonry (**D**). Although it was probably covered, no trace is left of the roof supports. To the northwest,

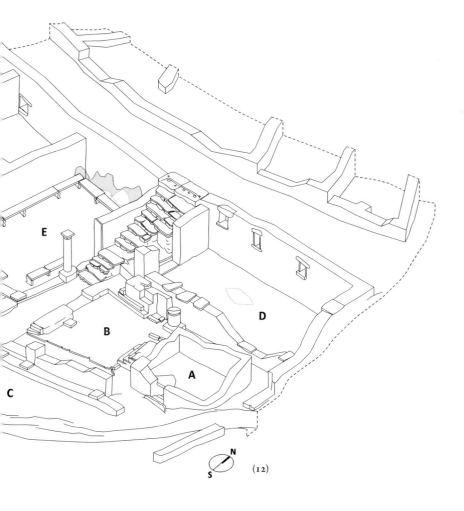

(12)

Egyptian cults and sanctuaries on Delos

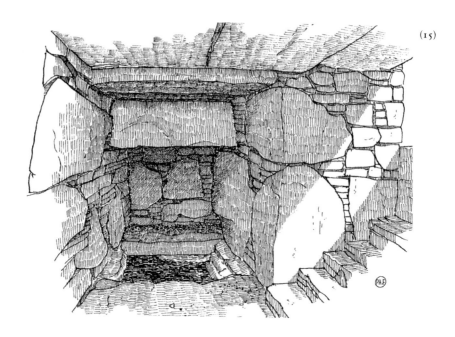

(15)

(16)

Three sanctuaries to visit

a second, irregularly shaped room was furnished with marble benches, found scattered about by excavators in the early 20th century (**12**, **E**; **16**). Dedicated to Sarapis, Isis and Anubis, these benches bear the names of their dedicators, and one still preserves traces of an engraved chequered pattern that probably served as a gameboard.

To the south was a third and final room (**C**) whose walls were almost entirely destroyed by the construction of a foundation wall supporting an aqueduct built probably in the 4th century AD to capture the waters of the Inopos. This subsequent installation was demolished by excavators in the early 20th century and the successive disturbances in this portion of the sanctuary make its organisation difficult to interpret. It is nevertheless possible to re-establish the general plan of this southern room, which opened onto the courtyard through a colonnade, partially obstructed by a wall erected on the courtyard side of the columns.

As recent excavations have confirmed, this small sanctuary was built by Apollonius, the author of the Chronicle, in the late 3rd or early 2nd century. Although the vast majority of dedications found here date from the first years of the 2nd century, it continued to be used throughout the entire Hellenistic period. It appears not to have been abandoned before the beginning of the 1st century, when the island, subject to military incursions by Mithridates' troops, was to a certain extent deserted and ceased to be a stopping point in Mediterranean traffic. No traces of worship or transformations can be clearly identified after the year 69.

SARAPIEION B

The Sarapieion B constructions (★) are located on the hill overlooking the Inopos reservoir (**17**). They are accessible from a narrow entrance located between two shops opening onto the street bordering the reservoir to the east. This entranceway was furnished with two marble benches, one of which still remains today: situated against the north wall on the left-hand side of the entrance, it bears a dedication to the Egyptian deities. The entryway leads to a staircase that provides access to the sanctuary's rooms (**18**). Landings on this stairway lead, on the south side, to a small room whose walls have almost entirely collapsed; and on the north side to a large square room, or more probably, a courtyard. Its unique layout consists of three small compartments, each about two metres wide, in its western section. It is possible that these chambers, separated by walls, or

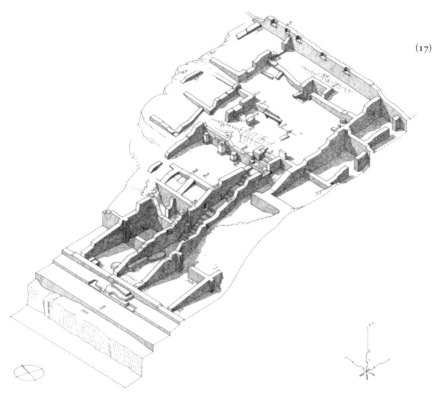

(17)

(18)

Three sanctuaries to visit

at least low walls (today razed), were chapels constructed to contain the statues of Sarapis, Isis and Anubis. Against the east wall of the courtyard and facing each of the compartments, stood three altars dedicated to the sanctuary's gods by the members of several Isiac associations. The two additional altars visible today were placed here after excavations (**19**).

Continuing further east, the staircase leads to a courtyard, onto which, as in Sarapieion A, open several rooms and a temple. The temple's marble facade catches the eye as it contrasts sharply with the other fairly dilapidated walls, all built from the rubble of miscellaneous materials (**20**). However, it is also very damaged, and about a third of the facade is missing. In front of the temple and reaching its facade is a wall extended by two benches. Traces lead us to believe that similar benches may have been located in the courtyard's southwest corner, and others in the western section, which today no longer exists. All the evidence points to a layout intended to accommodate meetings of the faithful facing the main temple (**21**).

A long terrace occupies the eastern part of the courtyard, which was probably covered by a portico. Here, in this section, a semi-underground crypt (**22**), made accessible by a few steps, was constructed, but unlike the crypt found in Sarapieion A, it features no device for conveying water. Its flooring, however,

contains sherds of pottery immersed in a thick hydraulic mortar (now concealed under a layer of sand), which shows that water must have been stored there, and perhaps in jars. Situated in the courtyard's northeast corner, one last room is accessible from both the courtyard and the east portico and features a slightly raised floor.

Due to the limited number of inscriptions found in this sanctuary, its history is not known in any detail. Based on epigraphic indications, Pierre Roussel dated its construction to the early 2nd century. The excavation trenches in the sanctuary, however, showed that its constructions were not erected before the end of the 2nd century or the beginning of the 1st century. The establishment's function has also been questioned: the epigraphic texts collected come almost entirely from associative groups of the faithful, suggesting that Sarapieion B was in fact a clubhouse, as seen elsewhere on the island (*e.g.*, that of the Association of the Poseidoniasts of Berytos), rather than an actual sanctuary.

SARAPIEION C

The third Sarapieion (★), whose proportions are much greater than those of the other two establishments (**23**), was the public sanctuary of the Egyptian

gods on Delos. Built on the side of Mount Cynthus, the complex fans out over a vast artificially reinforced esplanade. Its monuments, and in particular the Temple of Isis (whose facade was reconstructed in the early 20th century), are clearly visible from the port and catch the eye of visitors arriving at Delos. Sarapieion C's architectural development was gradual, continuing from the time it was founded, perhaps around 190–180, when Sarapis was officially adopted by the Delians, through to the beginning of the 1st century, when it reached its apogee. It was no doubt gradually abandoned after the events of the year 69. While today, visitors usually approach the sanctuary from the north, following the signposted route from the museum, in antiquity the main entrance was through the monumental gate (**24, A**) situated at the site's southern end. Today only the foundation block remains. This *propylon** opened onto a vast trapezoidal esplanade bounded on its south, east and west sides by Doric porticoes (**B**), many blocks of which have been found. In the centre, a paved pathway (**D**) about 40 metres long and 5 metres wide, and decorated with alternating sphinx statuettes and altars (**11** and **25**), leads to an edifice (**C**) located at the southern end of the terrace. Turning its back on the sanctuary's main entrance, this building opens north towards this avenue of sphinxes and is comprised of a square room preceded by a vestibule. Although it presents a temple plan, excavations have revealed that its *cella* was entirely occupied by a well, which has since been backfilled, and was therefore a hydraulic construction.

The north courtyard, arguably the oldest part of the sanctuary and also the most littered with votive monuments and bases, was entered via the southern esplanade. On its south and west sides, the paved courtyard (**24** and **26**, **G**) was bounded by an Ionic L-shaped portico of which many blocks have remained intact. The existence of these columns, capitals and elements of the entablature has enabled its antique appearance to be reconstructed. Opening to the south, the Temple of Sarapis (**F**; **27**) was situated on the northern side of the courtyard. Judging by its architectural features, it appears to date from the early 2nd century and probably prior to 167. In the courtyard facing the temple, the walls of an altar (**33**) can still be detected. To the east of this, a number of buildings, including the now restored Temple of Isis (**24** and **26**, **I**; **28**), stood on a rocky terrace nearly two metres above the level of the courtyard. Almost all the blocks of its

(**24**)

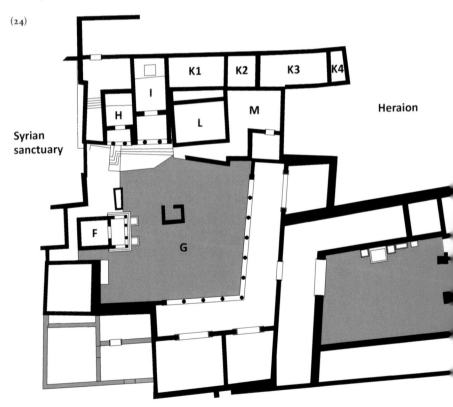

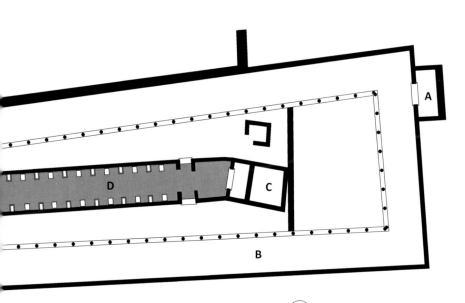

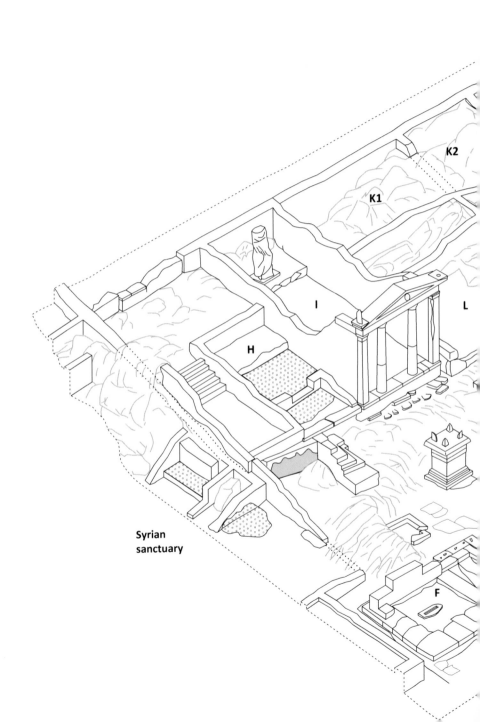

K2

K1

I

L

H

Syrian
sanctuary

F

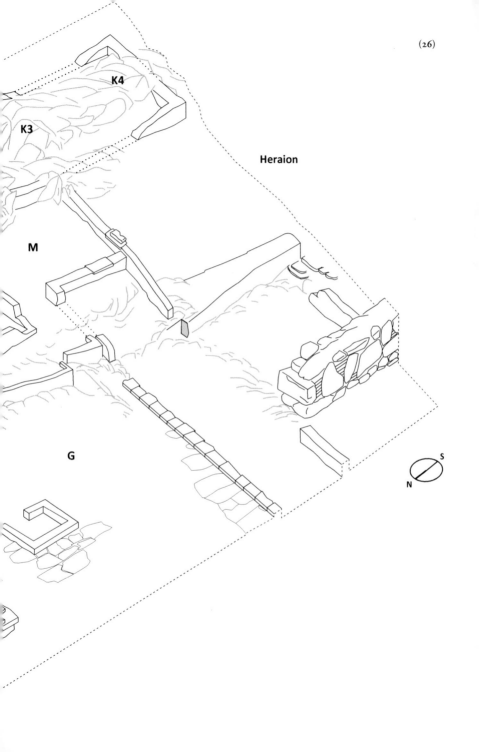

K4

K3

Heraion

M

G

S

N

facade have been preserved and, as revealed in the inscription engraved on the architrave, the Athenians were responsible for its foundation. The statue of the goddess has been replaced on the remains of its base (7) and its dedication dates from the year 128–127, most probably the approximate date of the temple's construction. On either side of this edifice stand constructions difficult to identify: to the north are the ruins of another chapel (**24** and **26, H**), possibly dedicated to Anubis; to the south, a group of very damaged rooms (**K, L, M**) sometimes identified as a *pastophorion** mentioned in texts. However, nothing is known of the activities that occurred there.

With the notable exception of the Temple of Sarapis in the northern courtyard, the majority of buildings visible in Sarapieion C date only back to the second half of the 2nd century, and even the beginning of the 1st century concerning the construction of the southern terrace. Although a few razed vestiges visible here and there attest to the existence of older constructions, it is impossible to

(27)

establish a coherent picture of the ensemble prior to the end of the 2nd century. Yet it is known that the sanctuary was operating as early as 190–180. In fact, nothing is known of the organisation during the Period of Independence or at the beginning of the Athenian domination, and the ruins currently visible are those of the sanctuary's final state, between the years 130 and 69.

(28)

Three sanctuaries to visit

(29)

Cult practices and administration

The cult's administration has been largely understood through the epigraphic texts discovered during the excavation of the three Sarapieia. They are however less informative about religious festivals, ceremonies and sacrifices. The current hypotheses regarding these subjects are based primarily on the observation of architectural vestiges and the furniture that has survived. It can also be assumed that cult practices attested in other Iseia or Sarapieia in Greece or Hellenistic Egypt (traces of which were later found in Italy: **29**) also took place on Delos.

CULT STAFF AND DEVOTEE ASSOCIATIONS

Each of the three Sarapieia had their own organisational methods for the worship of Egyptian deities. In the private Sarapieion A sanctuary the priesthood was hereditary and, as indicated in the Chronicle of Apollonius (box 1), had no term limit. Another inscription, probably dating from 164, mentions a priest named Demetrius of Rheneia who was presumably a descendant of Apollonius, and possibly even his son as he bears a patronymic name. The text is the transcription of a *senatus consultum** which authorizes the priest of the Sarapieion to remain in Delos after the Athenians' decree to expel its inhabitants (box 2). His ownership of the sanctuary as a descendant of Apollonius was presumably the reason for being granted such permission. Mention is also made of a Demetrius, otherwise known as Telesarchides of Delos, and a 'Demetrius, son of Demetrius' in the dedications. Judging by their names, it would appear that the priests of Sarapieion A were all recruited from the same family, though the order of succession is difficult to establish.

It was likely that the priest was assisted in his officiation by attendants. It is known that a 'person in charge of cures' for example existed, though details such as the exact date or whether he served on a permanent or occasional basis are unclear. He was, in any case, of Egyptian origin as his name was Horos son of Horos and he came from Kasion.

Engraved in Sarapieion A, this text is a copy of the Roman Senate's decision authorising the Sarapis priest to continue to serve the cult. It is dated from around 164, shortly after the Delians were expelled in 167.

The Strategi to Charmides, curator of Delos, greetings. After a long discussion in the boule about the decree of the Senate which Demetrius of Rhenea brought from Rome in reference to matters pertaining to the Serapeum, it was resolved not to forbid him to open and to tend the shrine as before and to write to you that you may know about this matter. We append the copy of the Decree of the Senate brought by him.

The praetor Quintus Minucius, son of Quintus, consulted the Senate in the Comitium on the intercalary Ides. Publius Porcius, son of Publius, Tiberius Claudius, son of Tiberius, of the tribe Crustumina, and Manius Fonteius, son of Gaius, assisted in drafting the decree. Whereas Demetrius of Rhenea requested that he should be allowed to tend the Shrine of Serapis on Delos and that the Delians and the Athenian governor should be restrained from forbidding his cult service, the senators proposed as follows in regard to the said matter:

Whereas he tended the shrine previously, insofar as we are concerned, he may continue to tend it, provided that nothing is done in opposition of the decree of the Senate. The proposal passed.

ID 1510

Translation: A. C. Johnson, P. R. Coleman-Norton, F. C. Bourne, *Ancient Roman Statutes* (1961), no. 33.

(2) *The* senatus consultum *of Delos*

More is known about the clergy of Sarapieion C due to the wealth of epigraphic findings. Following the usual procedures of Greek worship, the priests of Sarapis were replaced annually, and as their names were used to date the deposit of the offerings (box 3), they appear in almost all the dedications. They were also included in the list of Delos priesthoods during the second Athenian domination, and from this same period our sources cite other additional offices, including those of *kanephoros*, kleidouchos*, uphiereus*, oneirokrites*, zakoros*, aretalogos** and *lampterophoros**. Among what appears to be the numerous and specialised staff engaged in serving the Egyptian gods in the public sanctuary, some were responsible for specific duties performed in the Isiac cults (*e.g.*, the *aretalogos*, the *lampterophoroi* and the *oneirokrites*). Other functions also existed in Delos' Greek sanctuaries, *e.g.*, the *neokoros** during the Period of Independence and the *kanephoroi* and the *zakoros* under the second Athenian domination.

While nothing is known about the priests of Sarapieion B, a number of inscriptions found in the establishment evoke the associations that met there. Mention is made of *dekadistai* and *dekadistriai, enatistai, eranistai* and *sarapiastai*, as well as the *therapeutai* who also appeared in Sarapieia A and C, and the *melanophoroi* also attested in Sarapieion C. Only the *therapeutai* and the *melanophoroi* continue to be mentioned in the texts discovered in Sarapieion C after 167. The others either disappeared or ceased to engrave inscriptions.

The exact activities, organisation and composition of these associations are not entirely clear, and their structures vary in each of the three sanctuaries. Some present an established hierarchy, as in Sarapieion B, where the *koinon* of the *enatistai* was chaired by an *archithiasites** assisted by a secretary (*grammateus*). Others, such as the *therapeutai* in Sarapieion A, appear to have a more informal arrangement. They may simply have been worshippers who frequented the shrine and assembled for special events, led by a member chosen to collect donations. The terms customarily used to designate constituted groups, *koinon* or *thiasos*, have not been found in relation to them. On the other hand, the *therapeutai* of Sarapieion C seem to have formed a genuine *koinon*.

Membership of an association does not seem to have been exclusive – the *archithiasites* of the *enatistai*, for example, was also a *therapeutes* at Sarapieion A, while his secretary claimed the additional title of *melanophoros* – and the groups occasionally performed common acts of worship, as indicated in a dedication associating the *koinon* of the *therapeutai*, that of the *melanophoroi*, and the *thiasos* of the *sarapiastai*. Some, like the *dekadistai*, also accepted women (*dekadistriai*). The religious activities of these associations remain unknown, and at most, a few hypotheses can be deduced from their names. The *dekadistai* and *dekadistriai*, for example, met and held their celebrations on the tenth day of the month, and the *enatistai* on the ninth. The *melanophoroi*, who apparently played a more important role after 167, may have worn black dress in commemoration of Isis' mourning. It is possible that the *eranistai* organised banquets, as the term *eranos* designates the participation contributed by each member; the texts also mention a collective offering of banquet couches by the members of this *koinon*. In the versified section of the Chronicle of Sarapieion this use is also mentioned. While no banquet hall has been specifically identified in the Sarapieia, the rooms or outdoor spaces furnished with benches could possibly have been used for these feasts. It is also possible that if the diners reclined for the banquets, wooden beds would have been used, which have left no traces today.

Cult practices and administration

DEDICATIONS AND OFFERINGS

Dedications and offerings not only teach us about the gods of the Sarapieia, they also provide valuable information about the devotees. The names and ethnic origins of the dedicators, for instance, reveal that they were not especially connected to Egypt. Only a few, most of whom are women, bear such distinctly Egyptian names as Thermouthris, Taesis or Taessa. During the Period of Independence, apart from Apollonius the Elder, who arrived from Memphis with his god, the

In Sarapieion C, many offerings dedicated to the gods by private individuals were indicated by the dedications attesting to these devotional practices. The following choice of inscriptions involves the dedication of walls and a staircase financed by a private individual (ID 2098) and two texts engraved, respectively, around 140 on a white marble base (ID 2131) and around 90 (ID 2104). This latter dedication associates a local deity bearing the name of Zeus Kynthios, 'the Zeus of Mount Cynthus', with Isis and Sarapis.

In compliance with an order from Sarapis, Isis, Anubis, and Aphrodite, Apollonius, son of Asclepiodorus, in his own name and in the name of his wife Aphrodisia and his children Asclepiodorus, Apollonius, and Protimus, dedicated the staircase and the walls reaching the temple, under the priesthood of Zenon, son of Discourides, from the deme of Lamptrai.

ID 2098

To Sarapis, Isis, Anubis, Apollo, and Harpocrates, gods who share the same temple and the same altar, Eucles, son of Eucles, of Soloi, in his own name and in the name of his son.

ID 2131

To Zeus Kynthios, Sarapis and Isis, in compliance with an order, Neoptolemus, son of Philonides, under the priesthood of Dikaius, son of Dikaius, from the deme of Ionidai; Eukrates, son of Dionysius, grandson of Seuthes was *kleidouchos*; Apollonius, son of Dikaios was *zakoros*.

ID 2104

(3) *Dedications from Sarapieion C*

faithful were mostly Greeks, including both native Delians and citizens from other city-states. After 167, the diversity of their origins reflects that of the island's population, counting a throng of Athenians, Italians, Hellenised Orientals and Greeks from all over the Hellenic world. Most are known from the dedications or, in the case of the public sanctuary, from inventories, while other names appear on the lists of subscribers to the various Sarapieion C constructions. Some were probably passing merchants, but others obviously settled permanently in Delos as records naming them have been found in public documents as well as in the island's other sanctuaries. It is difficult to prove whether any of these migrants were familiar with Egypt as the Isiac cults were widespread throughout the Mediterranean basin. So, while it is possible that they were already acquainted with them in their homelands, they may also have discovered them on their arrival on Delos, attracted by the healing powers of the island's deities.

Although most of the offerings testifying to the piety of the faithful have disappeared, the epigraphic texts do give us an idea. Among these offerings, sculptures seemed to have been the most popular, particularly in Sarapieion C, testified by the number of bases (often the only remains) found in the sanctuary,

(30)

Cult practices and administration

together with inventory references. A few fragments however have been preserved, including the splendid statue of the Athenian woman Diodora, which today stands near the entrance to the avenue of sphinxes (30). This portrait, dedicated to Sarapis, Isis and Anubis by her husband and children was exhibited in an architectural niche, the blocks of which have survived. Works of bronze also seem to have been abundant in this sanctuary as the bases which supported them show the characteristic cavities in their upper surface. Dedications lead us to believe that several of them were portraits of priests or followers of the Egyptian gods. Administrators' inventories reveal that in addition to the statuary, the sanctuaries also contained valuable objects such as jewellery and precious metal work. Only a few traces are left of other more insignificant elements such as simple statuettes, small votive tablets or items of clothing. The quantity and diversity of these gifts testify to the piety of the devotees and the appeal of the Isiac cults on Delos. On the island, apart from the Sanctuary of Apollo, Sarapieion C was the establishment that received the most offerings during the 2nd century. In 179, the sums collected in its *thesauros* (offertory box) amounted to fifteen drachmas, compared to three drachmas, one and a half obols for Asclepius, and three obols for Aphrodite.

ALTARS AND SACRIFICES

Like the island's other deities, the Egyptian gods of Delos were honoured with periodic sacrifices. Although it is not known when and how these rituals were performed, a number of inscriptions mention contributions 'for the altar' and the faithful who assembled 'for sacrifices (*thysia**) and libations'. These indications refer to the money collected from devotees for the organisation of celebrations and show that such practices were common in the Sarapieion C.

The various altars discovered in each of the sanctuaries provide us with information on sacrificial practices. The circular or parallelepiped marble *bomoi** still occasionally preserve the dedications referencing the names of those who offered them. This is the case for those of Sarapieion B already cited. These *bomoi* are included in the category of so-called 'horned' altars, designating the small marble protuberances attached to the corners of their top surface or carved all in one for the smallest examples. Many were found in the Sarapieia B and C, including one situated below the Temple of Isis (24 and 26, I) in the northern courtyard of Sarapieion C (31), whereas none were found in Sarapieion A. Of Syrian

Egyptian cults and sanctuaries on Delos

origin, they are attested in Egypt from the 4th century and are also particularly
common in Isiac shrines beyond the Nile Valley. They are generally associated
with the widespread practice of perfume or incense burning in Egyptian cults.
The versified section of the Chronicle of the Sarapieion alludes to this burning
ritual for the god, and perfume oil burners and incense boxes are also listed in
the inventories of Sarapieion C; miniature perfume oil burners made of terracotta
or stone (32) were effectively found during excavations.

Other altars bear witness to the existence of blood sacrifices in the Sarapieia
of Delos. *Escharai** or 'pit altars' built in Sarapieion C consisted of enclosures
whose exterior walls contained the hearth's ashes mixed with sacrificial residue.
One such altar was unearthed during early excavations in the northern courtyard
(24 and 26, G) facing the Temple of Sarapis (33). Another two, located on the
southern terrace, have been the subject of more recent exploration. Study of the
bone remains found in the altar has revealed that the animals, for the most part
roosters, were offered to the sanctuary's gods as holocaustic* sacrifices. While
such practice was often associated with chthonic deities, it was also appropriate
for healing and saviour gods such as Sarapis and Isis on Delos. Furthermore,

Egyptian cults and sanctuaries on Delos

the Sarapieion C inventories mention an *escharon* – designating the building containing an *eschara* – as early as 156–155. This *escharon* therefore perhaps housed the *eschara* situated in the northern courtyard, which appears to be the oldest, as the two southern altars can be dated to the end of the 2nd century or the beginning of the 1st century.

Sarapieion A contains a masonry altar built against the wall of the courtyard that still preserves signs of its protective plastering (34). Its complex appearance is the result of the gradual addition of several votive bases to the central body of the *bomos*. These bear witness to the custom of placing offerings in the most favourable position to establishing relations with the gods. Whether or not the altar hosted only perfume burning rituals or whether animal victims were also consumed is not known. Judging however from its similarity to the altars dedicated to the cult of *Lares Compitales* on Delos, its form lends itself to blood sacrifices. We know that during the Compitalia festival piglets were sacrificed; these were only partially burned and the other part was probably consumed by the participants. It is therefore possible that animal sacrifices also took place in Sarapieion A, but which species were dedicated to the sanctuary's gods is a mystery.

REMARKABLE CONSTRUCTIONS:
THE SARAPIEIA'S CRYPTS AND WELLS

Water reservoirs situated in the heart of the sanctuaries were found in all three of Delos' Sarapieia. In Sarapieia A and B the crypts are still visible, but the large well located in the south terrace of Sarapieion C was backfilled after excavation. It is difficult to associate these installations with any particular cultic practice, although many hypotheses have been advanced. Apparently specific to Egyptian cults, these unique constructions have no equivalent on the island, but can be compared to constructions discovered in other sanctuaries devoted to Isis or Sarapis: hydraulic crypts are attested in Crete at the Iseion in Gortyne, in Pompeii in Italy, and in Belo in Spain.

In the 3rd century, Callimachus described the local legend which depicted the Inopos as a resurgence of the Nile, in his *Hymn to Delos*. The water from the Sarapieion A well, located in the immediate vicinity of the stream, could thus be regarded as sharing the waters of the prestigious Egyptian river. It has been suggested that this well could be interpreted as a kind of Nilometer meant to symbolically reproduce the annual flooding of the Nile in festivals similar

Cult practices and administration

to those held in Egypt. This assumption, however, seems a little far-fetched, especially as there is no evidence of flood festivals on Delos. More plausible is the idea that the waters of this installation and the hydraulic facilities in Sarapieia B and C were considered holy or sacred and perhaps even assimilated to those of the Nile.

The water from these reservoirs may also have been used for the cures conducted in Sarapieia A and C (there is no evidence to their existence in Sarapieion B). It was generally considered that water had a curative power in healing sanctuaries and the healing abilities of Sarapis and Isis already mentioned are well attested by inscriptions and a variety of offerings. However, as the methods used in the Sarapieia to treat the sick are unknown, it is impossible to determine whether or not water played an important role.

The water may also have been used for purifications, and perhaps even for daily rituals similar to those performed in Egypt. Here again, we lack elements confirming the existence of this kind of practice on Delos, and the amount of water they required does not seem to account for the complexity of the constructions; simple wells would have been sufficient.

The substantial water reserves located directly below the temples in Sarapieion A and Sarapieion C may indicate the existence of a specific water cult in these sanctuaries. This theory is plausible for the case of Sarapieion C, where the large well (**24**, **C**) located south of the avenue of sphinxes could be the *hydreion* mentioned in inscriptions. A god named Hydreios (*i.e.*, the deification of water) is also attested in this sanctuary. The avenue of sphinxes, which leads to the well, is specifically dedicated to this divinity together with Sarapis, Isis, Anubis and Harpocrates. While no such convincing evidence exists for the Sarapieia A and B, the location of the Sarapieion A well under the temple of Sarapis and accessible from the crypt may suggest cultic worship of its holy water in this sanctuary also.

The veneration of water is chronicled in the 2nd century AD text by Apuleius (*Metamorphoses*, XI, 11, 4), who alludes to the urn where it was contained. A number of Italian images depicting Isiac processions present one of the officiants carrying a vase comparable to the one described by Apuleius (**35**); and a fresco from Herculaneum, depicting the faithful assembled in an Isiac sanctuary facing a priest standing on the podium of the temple and presenting them with a vase (**29**), may also represent this water cult. Similar practices may have occurred in Delian sanctuaries, but caution is required as no distinct document is available

Egyptian cults and sanctuaries on Delos

for either the Hellenistic period or Delos. There is no reason either that such hypotheses concerning the use of these remarkable hydraulic devices are mutually exclusive. Water could well have been the object of cultic worship at the same time as it was used for purification rituals and/or therapeutic acts.

AN EXOTIC TOUCH

At first sight, the Sarapieia of Delos resemble other Delian constructions from the same period, presenting virtually no exotic features. The temples in Sarapieion C – and that of Isis in particular, which has been reconstructed since its excavations – evoke the Hellenised character of the cult. This is also true, as we have seen, of the sacred statuary and the sanctuaries' religious administration. The priests of Sarapieion C were Greek, and while Sarapieion A retained a hereditary priesthood, this was no doubt due to its private status as much as the Egyptian origin of the cults celebrated there. Notwithstanding the fact that, artistically and religiously speaking, the Sarapieia remained Greek sanctuaries, a few deliberate touches of exoticism can be noted. As already evoked, certain specialised functions among the cultic staff of Sarapieion C undoubtedly added an oriental touch to the rituals and periodic festivities celebrated within its walls. The architecture and furniture of this same sanctuary also exhibited other signs of an Egyptian nature, of which the avenue of sphinxes is the most obvious example.

Cult practices and administration

Dating from around the year 90, the dedication of the 'avenue of sphinxes' is preserved in two examples which were probably displayed on either side of its entrance; in it, several members of the Sarapieion C clergy are mentioned. The constructions are dedicated to Sarapis, Isis, Anubis, Harpocrates and Hydreios, a hydric divinity attested several times in the sanctuary and who is manifestly associated with the large well that is identifiable with the hydreion *mentioned in the inscriptions, and to which the avenue leads. In addition to the sphinxes, the dedication refers to other elements, notably the paving and altars, which are still visible, and the clock which has never been found.*

A certain (Demetrius?), son of Nicias [of Alexandria?], *melanephoros*, in his own name and in the name of his wife, Patrophila, his children, Nicias and Apollonia, and his relative Cleon, son of Cleon, dedicated at his own expense the altars, the paving, the sphinxes and the clock to Sarapis, Isis, Anubis, Harpocrates and Hydreios, under the priesthood of Artemidorus, son of Apollodorus, of the deme of Lamptrai; Theophilus, daughter of Artemidorus of the deme of Lamptrai was *kanephoros*; Euodos was *zakoros*.

ID 2087 and *ID* 2088

(4) *Dedication of the 'avenue of sphinxes'*

This paved avenue's dedication reveals that it was laid at the beginning of the 1st century, perhaps around 90, and although the same text has been conserved in two separate plaques, the name of the dedicator has disappeared (box 4). Carved from a greyish-coloured marine limestone rarely used for sculpture, four incomplete examples of the sphinx statuettes that adorned this path have survived (36); despite their damage, it is clear that they wore Egyptian style wigs. Although their placement is uncertain, it is supposed that they occupied the rectangular bases which alternate with the square shaped blocks presumed to be the altars mentioned in the dedication. Whatever its exact form, a path lined with sphinxes clearly constitutes a reference to Egypt and added a touch of exoticism to an otherwise Hellenistic sanctuary.

The furnishings of the sanctuaries also included a series of *aegyptiaca*, a term designating both genuine Egyptian objects and locally produced imitations. A splendid statuette of a dancer, dating from the 30th dynasty or the beginning of the Ptolemaic period (37) from the town of Sais, with no connection

to Delos or the Isiac cults, must have been brought back from Egypt and left as an offering in the sanctuary by a devotee fond of exoticism. On the other hand, the female statuette found in Sarapieion C, of which only the feet and the lower legs enclosed in a flat tunic have been preserved, is a good example of an Egyptian-like object most likely produced in Delos by a local craftsman familiar with Egyptian aesthetics (8). The same applies to the avenue of sphinxes and the statuette of Anubis already mentioned (10).

The inventories suggest that from the beginning of the 2nd century other genuine Egyptian or Egyptian-like images may have been kept in Sarapieion C. Two gilded wood statues or statuettes exhibited in wooden *aediculae*, probably in the form of a temple, were recorded in the Temple of Isis in 156–155. Both the technique and the presentation are derived from Egyptian traditions.

Personal devotion

As yet, only the elements of Egyptian worship linked to the Sarapieia and the established religion – even when this religion was practiced within the context of a private sanctuary or specific devotee associations – have been broached. Discoveries in the town of Delos however testify to the adoption of the Isiac gods by the island's population. These objects and inscriptions may represent a sign of personal devotion and even the existence of domestic cults. If the Chronicle text can be believed, Sarapis was first celebrated in the abode of Apollonius the Egyptian, before a sanctuary devoted to the god was constructed. Although this account must be interpreted with caution, the archaeological site of Delos has revealed the presence of the gods of the Isiac circle in Delian houses throughout the 2nd century and the beginning of the 1st century.

ISIACA IN HOUSES AND TOMBS

A great number of statues, statuettes, jewellery, amulets and inscriptions were found in the living quarters of Delos. As the majority of these objects were discovered during early excavations, their original placement is not always certain. Furthermore, as some may have been on sale in the town's shops or workshops, they cannot all be systematically associated with domestic worship. Such a supposition is supported by a relief discovered in a shop in the Agora of the Italians (★, 3) depicting Isis Pelagia. Others, such as the dedication discovered in the staircase of the Inopos reservoir (★), may have been taken from shrines and re-used in houses or other buildings. Nevertheless, certain pieces, including a dedication to Sarapis, Isis and Anubis found in a house near the Agora of Theophrastus (★), and another from a house located not far from the museum, are considered proof of domestic worship. This same observation can be made regarding the Egyptian or Egyptian-like subjects of terracotta statuettes whose uncertain place of discovery make their purpose difficult to understand.

Although their context remains unclear, these objects testify to the place and popularity the Egyptian gods enjoyed among the Delian population. Discovered in a house near the altar of Dionysus (★), a relief presents an original combination of Isiac symbols and Dionysiac themes (38). A front view shows a man dressed in a short tunic holding a *thyrsus** in his right hand. Beside him, and occupying the centre of the image, is a headdress composed of two feathers standing erect on a sun disc placed between two cow horns. Under this, intertwined ears of wheat are tied with ribbons. Further to the right, stands another, slightly shorter *thyrsus*. It is thought that the image may express the personal beliefs of the house's inhabitants.

In the House of Fourni, situated in the Delian countryside, several sculpted reliefs presenting religious subjects have been found, notably two Isiac headdresses (A 6994; A 4019: 39) and a banquet scene (A 4014). These objects were, however, found among other images unrelated to Egyptian cults, and the function of the building itself is a matter of debate. It has been thought that this large house may have been a clubhouse, particularly as several masonry and stucco altars, potentially used for religious celebrations, were identified in the main courtyard. If this were the case, the reliefs would testify to the particularly eclectic religious attachments of the association's members.

In the necropolis of Delos, located on the island of Rheneia, several tombs have also revealed elements which indicate that the deceased worshipped the Isiac gods. Among the terracotta statuettes was the more important find of a tomb containing a superb example of a bronze sistrum* (40). This ceremonial object

(38)

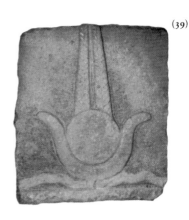
(39)

was an attribute of the goddess Isis and characteristic of Egyptian cults. The person entombed here seems to have shown particular allegiance to the goddess and has sometimes been considered an Isis devotee or priest. A funerary stele discovered at Aegina, but most probably originally from Rheneia, presents decoration consisting of a sistrum and a small box closed with a lid similar to one found on an Isiac stele in Athens. The stele belonged to a couple, Kerdon son of Rhodon and Parthenis, who it is supposed worshipped the Egyptian gods or, at least, the goddess Isis. Dating from the 1st or 2nd century AD, during the Roman era, this stele proves the lasting attachment to the Egyptian cults by the population who remained on Delos after the 'catastrophes' of 88 and 69, which saw the departure of many inhabitants.

(40)

Apart from the sanctuaries specifically devoted to them, the wealth of references to the Egyptian gods on Delos once more emphasises their normality: they are neither marginal nor exotic, and on the contrary form an integral part of Delian religion. Furthermore, it is clear that these images coexisted with representations of Hellenic gods or other oriental deities in the houses and various contexts in which they were found. There is no doubt that the Egyptian gods were not a separate category, and on the contrary, blended into the religious fusion which characterised the island at the end of the 2nd century.

HARPOCRATES, A DOMESTIC DIVINITY

While on Delos the image of Harpocrates was particularly popular in personal and familial devotion, he occupied a more minor place in the Sarapis sanctuaries. Although from the end of the 2nd century his name appears regularly in the Sarapieion C dedications, no temple was devoted to him. It is thought that his statue may have stood in the *naos** of his mother, Isis, as according to an inventory dating from 145–144, the god had received a cloak, a tunic and a belt with a silver disc from a certain Hierokleia, which were kept in the goddess' temple. Although slightly marginal in the Delian sanctuaries, the young god is frequently attested in domestic iconography. Terracotta statuettes, most often of uncertain origin, show him wearing a *pschent** (sometimes in a corrupted, unclear form), holding the index finger of his right hand to his lips (**41**); his image also appears on ear pendants (**42**). These representations are consistent with the common iconography of Harpocrates in the Greek world.

Excavations on Delos have also yielded less conventional images of this god, all of which come from private context. Discovered in the 'commercial quarter' near the port of Delos in 1903, a statue of a young boy whose legs end in the form of a hermaic pillar has been identified as a representation of Harpocrates (**43**). In his left hand, the god holds a cornucopia, of which only the lower part remains, and in his hair, he wears a headband (*strophion*), another indication of his identity. A similar, but larger statue (A 4262), was also found in a private

dwelling known as the 'house on the hill'. The god is draped in a thick cloak and his feet are replaced by a pillar. Despite the statue's mutilated state, it can be assumed that its left hand also held a cornucopia as the remains indicate a similar gesture to that of the other statue. The face is that of a smiling, juvenile god and the hairstyle, composed of two bulging masses formed above the forehead with two locks falling to the shoulders on either side of the face, is worthy of attention. It is probably an adaptation of the lotus-shaped crown occasionally worn by Harpocrates, combined with the 'Libyan curls' that are a frequent characteristic of Alexandrian representations.

These two statues, along with other fragments possibly belonging to similar objects, present a very particular image of Harpocrates, other examples of which may have existed outside of Delos. They do however appear to be specifically Hellenistic in their creation, and perhaps even attributable to Delian workshops. Either way, they demonstrate the popularity of this child god and protector of the home, who was probably the object of quite special devotion on the island.

(42)

Personal devotion

Egyptian cults and sanctuaries on Delos

Conclusion

Among the towns of the eastern Mediterranean where Isiac cults were well established during the Hellenistic period, no other site facilitates researchers' work as much as Delos. Although work on the vast documentation revealed on Delos has not yet been completed, this overview should provide readers with an insight into the extensive range of questions raised by the Delian vestiges. Resumed in the early 2000s, the excavations conducted in each of the three sanctuaries have uncovered their share of new finds and occasional surprises, which further enrich our knowledge of the Delian pantheon, the administration of the cults, and the related religious practices. In addition to these specifically local aspects, the cosmopolitan nature of the island's population must once more be emphasised, as it were these people who frequented the Sarapieia and thus contributed to the circulation – particularly throughout Italy – of the beliefs associated with them.

Glossary

Archithiasites: head of a *thiasos*, *i.e.*, a religious association.

Aretalogy, aretalogos: hymn praising the virtues (*arete*) of the gods; person in charge of writing or reciting it.

Bomos (plur.: *bomoi*): Greek term commonly used in archaeology to designate an altar whose table is elevated by a more or less constructed or imposing structure. *Bomoi* may be modest-sized pieces of furniture or monumental constructions.

Cella: Latin term, used in architecture to designate the main room of a temple.

Eschara (plur.: *escharai*): 'hearth'. A term used to denote a type of altar, sometimes called a 'pit altar' or 'hearth altar', consisting of a hearth positioned on the ground or in a cavity. The *eschara* may be contained in a constructed enclosure: buildings known as *escharones* (sing.: *escharon*), designating these constructions, have been found on Delos.

Hathoric crown: headdress consisting of a sun disc surrounded by cow horns, occasionally surmounted by two feathers and combined with ears of wheat. It is a symbol of the Egyptian goddess Hathor, sometimes assimilated to the Greek divinity Demeter. The crown is also frequently associated with Isis, especially in connection with Isiac cults outside of Egypt.

Holocaust: religious sacrifice in which the animal offered to the god is completely consumed by fire, usually in an *eschara*.

Kanephoros: literally 'basket bearer'; young Athenian woman from a good family who participated in public worship. Little is known about their role in the cult of Sarapis; they were perhaps more specifically attached to that of Isis.

Kleidouchos: 'holder of the keys'. A task entrusted in Sarapieion C to an Athenian of good family. The title is not often encountered in Isiac sanctuaries other than on Delos. The *kleidouchos* was perhaps a guardian in charge of the surveillance of sacred goods; they have also been linked to the daily Egyptian ritual of opening the temples.

Lampterophoroi: torchbearers during nocturnal ceremonies associated with Isiac cults.

Naos: Greek term signifying 'temple'. Sometimes used, like the Latin word *cella*, to designate the most sacred part of a temple.

Neokoros: a priest's assistant. The incumbent was a Delian randomly chosen from among citizens and remunerated for his office. The title ceases to appear after 167 (*IG* XI, 1032).

Oneirokrites: dream-interpreter. The title first appears in the Sarapieion C inscriptions during the Period of Independence (*ID* 2071).

Pastophoros, pastophorion: category of priests or members of a devotional association (the term's meaning is a matter of debate); room used for their meetings (*ID* 2124; *ID* 2085).

Propylon: vestibule. In architectural vocabulary the term refers to the monumental entrance to a sanctuary.

Pschent: Greek term designating the double crown of the Egyptian pharaohs. The *pschent* was also worn by Harpocrates in the Hellenistic iconography of the deity.

Senatus consultum: a Roman Senate decree.

Sistrum: musical instrument. A sort of metallic rattle that was waved to produce a sound. Several ancient examples have been found, including one from a tomb in Rheneia. The instrument appears in a great number of images representing Isiac ceremonies (processions or festivities in the sanctuaries). It originated in Egypt where it was used in festivities honouring Hathor.

Theriomorphic: literally 'in bestial form'. Egyptian deities were frequently depicted in animal or semi-animal forms.

Thyrsus: in Greek imagery, the *thyrsus* is an attribute of Dionysus or his companions (maenads or satyrs). It is generally depicted as a long wooden stick tipped with a pine cone; the shaft is sometimes decorated with foliage (ivy or vines).

Thysia: term generally translated as 'sacrifice'. The Greek word *thysia* designates a ceremony where an animal is killed and then shared between gods and men: the part intended for the gods is burned on a *bomos*; the participants in the ceremony consume the remaining part.

Uphiereus: subordinate priest.

Zakoros: the *zakoros* acts as sacristan and assistant to the priest in Sarapieion C (*ID* 2104). It was an annual office, but at the beginning of the 1st century the same person served for eighteen years.

Further reading

Delos (general reading)

Ph. BRUNEAU *et al.* (eds.), *Délos, île sacrée et ville cosmopolite* (1996).

Ph. BRUNEAU, J. DUCAT, *Guide de Délos* (4th ed., 2005).

Cl. PRÊTRE *et al.*, *Nouveau choix d'inscriptions de Délos* : *lois, comptes et inventaires* (2002).

Isiac cults and gods (in Greece)

A. BERNAND, *Alexandrie des Ptolémées* (1995).

L. BRICAULT, *Les cultes isiaques dans le monde gréco-romain* (documents, translations and commentaries) (2013).

L. BRICAULT, *Isis Pelagia: Images, Names and Cults of a Goddess of the Seas* (2020).

Isiac cults and gods on Delos

M.-Fr. BASLEZ, *Recherches sur les conditions de pénétration et de diffusion des religions orientales à Délos (IIe-Ier siècle avant notre ère)* (1977).

P. ROUSSEL, *Les cultes égyptiens à Délos du IIIe au Ier siècle av. J.-C.* (1915–1916).

Specialist studies

C. E. BARRETT, *Egyptianizing Figurines from Delos: A Study in Hellenistic Religion* (2011).

H. BRUN-KYRIAKIDIS, 'L'exposition des statues-portraits dans le Sarapieion C de Délos', in R. VON DEN HOFF, Fr. QUEYREL, E. PERRIN-SAMINADAYAR (eds.), *Eikones, portraits en contexte : recherches nouvelles sur les portraits grecs du Ve au Ier s. av. J.-C.* (2016), pp. 65–87.

Egyptian cults and sanctuaries on Delos

Ph. Bʀᴜɴᴇᴀᴜ, 'Le Quartier de l'Inopos à Délos et la fondation du Sarapieion A dans un « lieu plein d'ordure »', in *Études déliennes* (1973), pp. 111–136.

Ph. Bʀᴜɴᴇᴀᴜ, 'Le *dromos* et le temple C du Sarapieion C de Délos', *BCH* 104.1 (1980), pp. 161–188.

M. Lᴇɢᴜɪʟʟᴏᴜx, H. Sɪᴀʀᴅ, 'Rituels sacrificiels et offrandes animales dans le Sarapieion C de Délos', in G. Eᴋʀᴏᴛʜ, J. Wᴀʟʟᴇɴsᴛᴇɴ (eds.), *Bones, Behaviour and Belief: The Zooarchaeological Evidence as a Source for Ritual Practice in Ancient Greece and Beyond* (2013), pp. 167–179.

J. Mᴀʀᴄᴀᴅᴇ́, *Au musée de Délos* (1969).

J. Mᴀʀᴄᴀᴅᴇ́, 'L'image sculptée d'Harpocrate à Délos', *Bulletin de la classe des beaux-arts* 71 (1989), pp. 242–276.

I. S. Mᴏʏᴇʀ, *Egypt and the Limits of Hellenism* (2011).

H. Sɪᴀʀᴅ, 'Le style égyptien et les échanges d'art dans les *Sarapieia* de Délos', *Revue d'archéologie moderne et d'archéologie générale* 14 (2001), pp. 133–148.

H. Sɪᴀʀᴅ, 'L'*hydreion* du Sarapieion C de Délos : la divinisation de l'eau dans un sanctuaire isiaque', in L. Bʀɪᴄᴀᴜʟᴛ, M. J. Vᴇʀsʟᴜʏs, P. G. Mᴇʏʙᴏᴏᴍ (eds.), *Nile into Tiber: Egypt in the Roman World* (2007), pp. 417–447.

H. Sɪᴀʀᴅ, 'Les sceaux du Sarapieion C de Délos', *BCH* 134.1 (2010), pp. 195–221.

Cited texts

List of illustrations

Map 1 — Delos, plan showing all the ruins of the main plain (from J.-Ch. Moretti [ed.], *Atlas*, 2015): location of Sarapieia and buildings mentioned in the text.

Map 2 — Delos, Inopos Quarter (from J.-Ch. Moretti [ed.], *Atlas*, 2015): location of the buildings mentioned in the text.

pp. 2–3 — View of the site of Delos in 1910 (Archaeological Society at Athens).

1. Column bearing the text of the Chronicle of the Sarapieion, photographed in Sarapieion A in 1912.

2. Bronze ears dedicated to Isis (Archetype 82, drawing Fr. Siard).

3. Relief from the Agora of the Italians representing Isis Pelagia [A 3187] (photo H. Brun-Kyriakidis).

4. Marble statuette of Isis bearing a cornucopia [A 378], found northwest of the House of Dionysus (photo Ph. Jockey).

5. Intaglio representing a cornucopia, found in the southern *eschara* of Sarapieion C (photo Ph. Collet; drawing Fr. Siard).

6. Statuette of Sarapis enthroned [A 1936], Sarapieion B.

7. Statue of Isis in Temple I, Sarapieion C (photo H. Brun-Kyriakidis).

8. Fragmentary Egyptian statuette [A 2148] with a dedication [*ID* 2145], Sarapieion C.

9. Seal imprint from the southern *eschara* of Sarapieion C: Hathoric crown (drawing Fr. Siard).

10. Fragmentary statuette representing Anubis [A 5280], Sarapieion A.

11. Avenue of sphinxes during excavations in 1909, Sarapieion C.

12. Sarapieion A, axonometry (drawing F. F. Muller).

13. Reconstruction of the Sarapieion A courtyard (drawing Fr. Siard).

14. Sarapieion A as seen from the south (photo H. Brun-Kyriakidis).

15. Interior of the crypt, Sarapieion A (drawing Ph. Fraisse).

16. Room furnished with marble benches, Sarapieion A (photo H. Brun-Kyriakidis).

17. Sarapieion B, axonometry (drawing N. Bresch).

18. Sarapieion B as seen from the west (photo H. Brun-Kyriakidis).

19. Courtyard with altars as seen from the north, Sarapieion B (photo H. Brun-Kyriakidis).

20. Forecourt temple and benches as seen from the south, Sarapieion B (photo H. Brun-Kyriakidis).
21. Reconstitution of the temple facade and the forecourt furnished with benches, Sarapieion B (drawing Fr. Siard).
22. The crypt, Sarapieion B (photo H. Brun-Kyriakidis).
23. Sarapieion C, aerial view taken from the north (photo C. Gaston).
24. General plan of Sarapieion C (drawing F. F. Muller).
25. Reconstitution of the avenue of sphinxes and the hydraulic construction, Sarapieion C (drawing Fr. Siard).
26. Axonometry of the north courtyard and the east terrace of Sarapieion C (drawing F. F. Muller).
27. Temple of Sarapis, Sarapieion C (photo H. Brun-Kyriakidis).
28. Temple of Isis, Sarapieion C (photo H. Brun-Kyriakidis).
29. Fresco found in Herculaneum representing an Isiac ceremony, Museum of Naples (Archetype 82, drawing Fr. Siard).
30. Statue of the Athenian woman Diodora, Sarapieion C (photo H. Brun-Kyriakidis).
31. Horned altar situated below the Temple of Isis, in the north courtyard of Sarapieion C (photo H. Brun-Kyriakidis).
32. Miniature altar with a dedication to Sarapis, Isis and Anubis (*ID* 1417), Sarapieion A.
33. Hollow altar (*escharon*?) in the north courtyard of Sarapieion C (photo H. Brun-Kyriakidis).
34. Masonry altar in the courtyard of Sarapieion A (photo H. Brun-Kyriakidis).
35. 'Mattéi relief' representing an Isiac procession (Archetype 82, drawing Fr. Siard).
36. Sphinx from the avenue of sphinxes (D), Sarapieion C (photo H. Brun-Kyriakidis).
37. Statuette of a dancer [A 379], Sarapieion C (photo Ph. Collet).
38. Isiac relief found near the altar of Dionysus [A 3181].
39. Relief representing an Isiac symbol [A 4019] from the House of Fourni (photo A. Guimier).
40. Bronze sistrum from a tomb in Rheneia.
41. Terracotta statuettes representing Harpocrates; the first [A 2429] was found in the cistern of the Palestra of the Lake; the other [A 2525] in the vicinity of the port.
42. Ring featuring a figurine of Harpocrates with an owl and a dog from the street known as the 'rue du Théâtre'.
43. Statue of Harpocrates, from the commercial quarter [A 4260] (photo Ph. Jockey).

Iconographic credits: EFA, unless otherwise stated.

Contents

Printed in September 2021
by n.v. PEETERS S.a.

ISBN: 978-2-86958-550-8

Legal deposit: 4th quarter 2021

Director: Véronique Chankowski – Publishing manager: Bertrand Grandsagne – Editorial follow up: EFA, Iris Granet-Cornée –
Graphic design, prepress: EFA, Guillaume Fuchs – Translation and editing of texts in english: Sally Ruddock Rivière